92 Seconds in the Nurses' Lounge - Devotionals for a Busy Shift

Jennifer Goolsby

Published by Jennifer Goolsby, 2022.

92 SECONDS IN THE NURSES' LOUNGE - DEVOTIONALS FOR A BUSY SHIFT

First edition. July 4, 2022.

Copyright © 2022 Jennifer Goolsby.

ISBN: 979-8201432140

Written by Jennifer Goolsby.

Welcome to the Nurses' Lounge

I KNOW IT HAS BEEN a while since you've seen this room. Sit back, relax, and let the Word refresh you and help you to face another shift.

I have been a nurse for over twenty-five years, so I've been where you are now. Trying to keep up with an ever-sicker patient load and feeling undervalued and overworked. In those times, it is easy to forget why you chose this profession at all.

Or you are a new nurse. You are full of excitement and anxiety about your first days away from the supervision of a clinical instructor or a preceptor. You know you need guidance and wisdom from the Great Physician now more than ever.

I certainly do not have all the clinical answers, nor all the spiritual answers. I have learned Who I can go to when I need help, though. In a quarter-century of nursing, I have worked in acute care settings and clinic settings, with the newly born, the very old, and everyone in between. I have cared for men and women of all skin tones, religions, political persuasions, and nationalities. There are a few truths that are universal to nurses in all settings, and across all country boundaries. For example, it was a rare day that I got to sit down for a full thirty-minute lunch when I worked in the hospital setting. Most days I ran to the bathroom right after receiving report because I knew that may be my only chance the whole shift. 92 seconds, that is all you get!

These days I am using my spiritual gift of nurse-encourager - it is in there, right under prophecy and giving! I hope in these pages you find a reason to keep pursuing excellence with the help of the Holy Spirit, in this world's second oldest profession for women. (The first better go unmentioned in a Christian book, don't ya know!)

Later at home, after a scrub-down and a beverage of your choice, you may wish to read the longer Bible passage.

I pray in these pages you will find laughter, sustenance, and joy. You rock, nurse friends o' mine, so keep on keepin' on!

With love,

Jennifer

Time to Quit "Eating our Young"

QUICK VERSE FOR THE nurses' lounge: "Don't let anyone look down on you because you are young, but set an example for the believers in speech, in conduct, in love, in faith, and in purity." 1 Timothy 4:12

For further study later: 1 Timothy 4

I ducked out of the nurses' lounge and hustled into the bathroom. My shift had just started, but the tears were already threatening.

Had a patient died? No. Had I made a mistake? Nope. Was I overwhelmed? Every shift as a new graduate nurse had moments of overwhelm, but I was feeling fairly good, overall. However, one senior night nurse was making it her mission to prove how I didn't know anything. She asked me nitty-gritty details in report, pointed out everything I missed, and shook her head if I hadn't mentioned it to her.

They were more knowledgeable about their disease than I was. Yet they never gave me a tough time when I slowly, laboriously went through their assessments or mispronounced an unfamiliar medication name.

This nurse, though! Every evening that I saw her coming I would groan to myself. She was making me dread work. I felt so stupid around her!

"Honey, look at me, please." Joanna, an older LVN on the unit, came in moments later.

It was my first job out of nursing school, and I loved my job. The kids I cared for had frequent admissions due to having chronic health conditions.

I wiped my eyes and turned to her.

"Don't let her ruin your joy or make you question your abilities as a nurse, you hear me?" She shook her finger at me, but she was smiling.

"She knows the kids don't like her so she tries to thrive in the only way she can - perfectionism. She is an amazing technical nurse, but it takes more than that to be a successful nurse. It also takes compassion – and you can't teach that! It comes from here." She pointed to her chest. "And you've got heart. If you need help or feel lost, you come to me or another trusted nurse, okay? It's tough to get your sea legs at first. Most of us understand that. Do not let the ones that don't understand cause you to doubt your worth."

Later, when I heard the term "nurses eat their young" I remembered that night shift nurse. Then I remembered Joanna and her sweet words. We are mentors to the generations behind us. We must teach technical skills, true, but let's also teach kindness and grace.

Lord, may I be an encouragement to the new nurses that I precept and work with every day. Help me to be their cheerleader and not expect perfection after their first few months. Remind me of how it feels to be on my own for the first time. Amen.

Here's to Trying New Things

QUICK VERSE FOR THE nurses' lounge: "See, I am doing a new thing! Now it springs up; do you not perceive it? I am making a way in the wilderness and streams in the wasteland." Isaiah 43:19

For further study later: Isaiah 43

Some of us are more heroic than others of us.

No, I'm not talking about Care Flight professionals who fly into what you know will be a train wreck (sometimes literally).

Or the Armed Forces medics treating the wounded in combat conditions.

Although they are studs in scrubs, I admit...

Yes, I'm referring to my brave colleagues who go back to school.

Okay, it's not exactly reattaching arms while bullets are flying overhead, but it's still BRAVE.

I tried once. I entered the school's website, perused course offerings,

gasped over the requirements, fainted over the price, and promptly closed the browser.

I thought of the hours of study, essay writing, and panic attacks and decided

I'm happy at my level of education, thank you. I don't mind getting certified in my specialty or taking ACLS, but NO MORE SCHOOL!

So, here's to the new mom who is spending her maternity leave trying to finish a course before she heads back to work, to the man juggling night shifts on ICU, a prn job as an EMT for the fire department, plus schoolwork, to the middle-aged nurse who can't remember why she came in here, but can recite the neural pathways to the such-and-such (I don't know - I didn't go back to school, remember?).

We raise our glasses to you. Three hip-hip-hoorays! May your study sessions be uninterrupted, your recall for exams mind-blowing, and your professors' grade curve be steep (or is it gently sloping? I can't remember). To those of us keeping the cheap seats warm, we rock, too. God gifted us with ability to keep on keepin' on, staffing our units, tending to our patients, working through staff shortages and lean days when we haven't had a pay raise for years.

If I am supposed to go back to school, regardless of how I *feel* about it, can you join me in praying for willingness? Thank you!

Lord, bless the nurses working long hours, caring for their homes, studying many hours, plus juggling this with school hours. I pray for wisdom and understanding for them, plus Your supernatural patience. I am thankful they are taking those steps, so we have intelligent nurse practitioners, nurse anesthetists, and hospital administrators. (Sorry, Lord, about the sarcasm You heard in that last one. Someone must do it. Might as well be a nurse who knows how things work in the trenches.) Help us to cheer them on or to volunteer for a shift when they need to study, and to be there clapping loudly when they graduate. Amen.

I Hate Being a Newbie

QUICK VERSE FOR THE nurses' lounge: "The steadfast love of the Lord never ceases; His mercies never come to an end; they are new every morning; great is Your faithfulness." Lamentations 3:22-23

For further study later: Lamentations 3

I am surrounded by teachers dressed in cute "teacher clothes" (no more comfy, but ugly scrubs!). They all know one another, have inside stories and jokes, know the ins and outs of district politics. I am on the outside looking in - part of them and yet far removed. Junior high girl all over again!

I have done this new job thing before, but it has been a while. Twenty years! I knew everyone before - from the housekeeper on my floor to the CNO, not that I saw her often!

Now I will have a principal and a district nurse manager, who I won't see often. I will have not only children, but also faculty and staff in my care.

The weight of the responsibility is daunting.

Okay, deep breath. Concentrate! Much of the things they are saying at the front of the room are gibberish to me. I imagine orientees felt that way at the hospital, with all the unique terminology and abbreviations. I need to write this stuff down and bring it to my manager to see how much of it applies to me.

Way in the back, at the edge of my consciousness, I hear that still, small

voice I have learned to listen to through the years. "I brought you here. You are more than capable and qualified. In those moments when you do not know what to do, turn to Me. I set the galaxies spinning and the tides rolling in and out. I am the Great Physician, the Healer, the Alpha, and Omega.

Trust me to help. You are my Beloved. Trust me with all of it."

I know, Lord, that You brought me to this new job. Thank You for the blessing of caring for children in their school environments. I trust you in the newness of this place. You are with me, just as surely as You were with me in my old job. Give me a clear mind as I prepare for what is ahead. Give me quick thinking as I take in new procedures and client base. Give me patience as I navigate new waters. Give me wisdom to ask for help when I am not sure of my next step. I could not do this without You! Amen.

If You're a Toe, be a Great One!

QUICK VERSE FOR THE nurses' lounge: "Having gifts that differ according to the grace given to us, let us use them, if prophecy, in proportion to our faith; if service, in our serving; the one who teaches, in his teaching; the one who exhorts, in his exhortation; the one who contributes, in generosity; the one who leads, with zeal; the one who does acts of mercy, with cheerfulness." Romans 12:6

For further study later: Romans 12

It's not until you can't use a toe that you realize how important it is.

My mom and my husband have had to limit the use of a toe recently, in a "boot" or surgery. It's amazing how that throws your gait off and causes hip and knee pain. They appreciate those appendages much more now.

Not long ago, both of our CNAs scheduled were out – one on maternity leave, one with the flu. Miracle of miracles, we had plenty of nurses, so I volunteered to take on the CNA role. How hard can it be?

Well! Let me just say that I have never been so "worned-out," as my youngest said when he was little.

It takes prioritizing, learning unknown storage areas, using muscles you never thought you had, and pulling out patience you *knew* you didn't have.

For those of you who do all your own patient care, God bless you.

And consider all the overlooked people — working as a pharmacy tech, running all over the hospital with stat meds, and being chewed out for "delaying" when you get there. Or as an orderly, needing to be on five units in ten minutes to transport patients. Or as an OR housekeeper, with five dirty rooms and grumpy surgeons following you around asking when Room 3 will be cleaned. (I have seen it!)

I don't know about your CNAs, but ours epitomize kindness, even on busy days. They are respectful of the elderly, patient with the woman requesting the same thing twenty-two times per shift, and smile and nod when we interrupt their present task to perform another. They are great at their "small" job!

Nurses have gotten so specialized and/or task-oriented that we ignore the contributions of those working behind the scenes to make us look good.

As I type this, it's Nursing Assistants Week. Where are the supportive memes and gift websites for them? Perhaps it is time for the nursing profession to celebrate them more.

I am ashamed of myself, Lord. Forgive me for taking our ancillary staff for granted. I guess you are teaching me humility today! May I express in my words, expressions, and actions how I value their input on our unit. When I am able, remind me to take some of their burden – quickly make a bed or stand nearby while my patient showers. Give me eyes to see and words to encourage when they need lifting up – on busy days or after a hard assignment. Bless them in ways I can't see – with a kind spouse or a sympathetic friend. Remind them in Your way that their work has value. Amen.

For Everything, a Season

———

QUICK VERSE FOR THE nurses' lounge: "He has made everything beautiful in its time. He has also set eternity in the human heart; yet

no one can fathom what God has done from beginning to end."

Ecclesiastes 3:11

For further study later: Ecclesiastes 3

Some days all of this feels too hard. I'm sure you know what I mean. I looked up the definition of burnout in the dictionary and I sometimes think I have them all.

- Dreading going to work - check

- Impatience and irritability with co-workers for no discernible reason - check

- Difficulty concentrating - check

- Lack of satisfaction with achievements - check

- Change in sleep habits - too much or too little - check

- Lack of energy to be productive - check

- Stress- related physical complaints—such as headaches, abdominal or bowel problems, generalized aching - check

- Sudden criticism of policies and procedures that have been in place for a long time - check

- Misuse of food, caffeine, alcohol, sleeping pills, etc. to make it "feel better" - check

So, where do I go from here? I miss the days of loving what I do, being excited to come to work, and looking forward to being with my colleagues.

I feel like I'm completely powerless to change my attitude, my frustration with my job, and even my schedule. Seniority seems to mean so little to this organization - so, why stay? Yep, that's where I am. Looking for a change. But is that what I really need? Help!

After griping with co-workers and perusing job boards, my mom (a once-upon a time nurse herself) reminded me of my desire to be a labor and delivery nurse. It won't be easy; it's a hard field to break into because those nurses love their jobs. Imagine! She also gently reminded me that there was a Person I should be talking to before everyone else.

Why is the last thing we do the first thing we should be doing? Instead of complaining about it, let's pray about it. The Lord knows us intimately. He knows our deepest desires and heart passions. Let's talk to Him.

Help, Lord! I need to know my next right step. Can you give me wisdom on whether to stay or go? I know there are seasons for things - You've made it that way - but I don't want to jump without a word from You. Maybe just start looking? Maybe take a vacation? Maybe see a counselor? I also want to be brave, not just stay here because it is what I know. Where could You be calling me next? I want my work to matter, not just be a J-O-B. Give me some direction, please, through Your Word or through others Amen.

I Screwed up, God

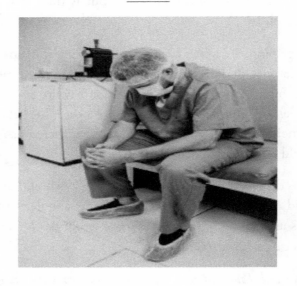

QUICK VERSE FOR THE nurses' lounge: "There is none righteous, no, not one." Romans 3:10

Further study for later: Psalm 51

I think I'm gonna be sick. How could I be so inattentive to make that med error? Even with all the safeguards I complain about All.Of.The.Time. I can't ever complain again.

Thank You, thank You that it happened to a young, healthy patient who could tolerate that dose. Thank You that I realized it quickly so we could take rapid steps to monitor her. Thank You that the doctor was sympathetic and proactive about it. Thank You that the patient was forgiving, once she was assured things were under control. Thank You that we could prevent tragedy from it - oh, sweet Jesus, what if we couldn't?!

I feel so ashamed, humiliated, and horrified.

Oh, God, but when others are understanding it really DOES make it better. Especially the older nurses who have each told me about their own stories of med errors.

"It's happened to me, too" can be the sweetest words ever. Although it does make me want to sob on their shoulders...

I need to remember that in the future when I am comforting another nurse who has had this happen to them.

I see why soldiers have Post Traumatic Stress Disorder. Not that this is the same as battle, but I think I will have flashbacks next time I pass meds.

Because it does happen. We are human, as much as the public would like us to be superhuman. No matter how many steps we take to assure that these occurrences are less, they still happen.

And yet, and yet... I never want it to happen to ME again. I never again want to feel that terror or experience that shame.

That is why the safeguards are there. Obviously, even when they are in place, humans can make mistakes.

This has been a wake-up call, for sure. I have become too complacent about medications and procedures that affect people's health.

*Help me, Lord. Help me to really pay close attention when I am **passing** my patients' meds. Remind me of this queasy feeling I have so that I am more cautious next time, and the next. Never let me take this step, or any step of patient care for granted, to become rote and unthinking. Help all of us to be mindful of what we are doing. Amen.*

Green-Eyed Monster

QUICK VERSES FOR THE nurses' lounge:" Whatever you do, work heartily, as for the Lord and not for men, knowing that from the Lord you will receive the inheritance as your reward. You are serving the Lord Christ." Colossians 3:23-24

For further study later: Exodus 35

It was one of those days. Not too busy, just steady. Not too much patient- or doctor- or coworker-drama. I even got a lunch break. After I finished scarfing down my food (a habit that is hard to break), I began to scroll through Facebook.

One of my friends posted a picture of lunch at Del Frisco Steakhouse, paid for by his company. Another friend posted a picture of herself with friends at brunch, after dropping off the kids at school. Another showed off her new, beautiful car. The old envy began to creep in.

"Must be nice. I have not had a raise to equal the cost-of-living increase in three years. My options for lunch are what I bring, the mediocre cafeteria food, or, on most days around here, a graham cracker and skim milk."

Man, they have nice lives. I cannot imagine his fun job – all the travel and hanging out with celebrities. She got that award for architect of the year". "None of them have to work next week!" (Yes, it was the holidays, the time of the year when nurses get more disgruntled than usual dover their choice of career.

Really, I am nothing more than a pill-pusher and task-charter. What made me think this would be a good idea?" Sigh...

My friend covering my patients for lunch popped her head in.

"Sorry to interrupt, but Mrs. Reingold insists that she wants only you to help her to the bathroom."

"Ok. Be right there." I took another swig of water before heading to room 224.

"Ah, Jennifer!" The elderly lady's eyes lit up when she saw me. "How lovely to see you!"

She just saw me twenty minutes ago, when I was in here for the twentieth time, I thought.

"You are the sweetest thing," she continued. "On the days you don't work, it just isn't the same. You are more patient than some of these people, giving me time to get out of bed and to the bathroom. I'm sorry. Were you in the middle of something?"

Ouch.

"No, ma'am. I always have time for you. Here, let me help you."

"Thank you. You girls - and boys now! – are just angels. Especially here. I know us old folks are hard to take care of. We can't hear, can't see, and take too long to potty!"

"It's a blessing, Mrs. Reingold."

And, Lord, it is. Forgive me for my poor-me attitude. Thank You for this career I've chosen, caring for those who can't care for themselves. Remind me again of the calling I had to nursing. If I can bring a smile to someone's face, if I can show a little extra patience, if I can ease someone's suffering with my pill-pushing, may I not despise it. Amen

Chewed up, Spit Out, & Stepped On

QUICK VERSE FOR THE nurses' lounge: "The next morning Jesus woke up very early. He left the house while it was still dark and went to a place where he could be alone..." (Easy Reader Version)

For further study later: Luke 4:42, Mark 6:32, Matthew 14:13, Mark 8:13, Luke 5:3

Let's face it. This is demanding work, y'all.

Yes, you will hear my Texas come out in this devo today. Somehow our over-the-top dialect is the only thing that does these sorts of days and weeks justice.

I could've used the term "compassion fatigue" to title this. But it is more than fatigue after a grueling day.

It's rode hard and put up wet.

It's goin' home with your dogs barkin' after many, many shifts.

It's one wheel down and the axle draggin.'

Okay, you get the point!

After we run twelve to fourteen hours at work, many of us come home to care for our own people. Children, spouses, aging parents, even pets. Plus, we have daily responsibilities that never end, even if we have family around to help shoulder the load.

-Laundry.

-Meal planning.

-Carpooling.

And no civilian better tell me "You only work three days a week!" or "You have a stretch of seven days off!", or whatever schedule you work. Nope!

Okay, hold on. Today's entry isn't about complaining. It's about taking time to care for yourself, so you don't burn out five years into your career.

Jesus knew all about this. He frequently got out by Himself to recharge.

Out on a boat, on a long walk, in a garden. He spent time communing with His Father and feeling the wind and salt spray in His face. Jesus knew how to appreciate the gifts of solitude and rest.

A wise counselor told me to intentionally practice self-care every day. It was a period when I was overwhelmed in every area - vocationally, relationally, and practically. She made me list thirty things that made me feel nurtured. It was hard coming up with them! Some were small - take a bubble bath. Some were big - take a vacation. Most were in-between.

Read two chapters of a favorite book.

Get a pedicure.

We choose how we respond to our fatigue. Do we let it boss us around, ordering us to either give up or only look out for number one? Or do we choose to do as Jesus did, when He could? Give ourselves space to recover, permission to relax, take a Sabbath to rest even if it isn't on Sunday because this is our weekend to work. We might have to get a sitter or take advantage of the day you're off while the kids are in school - to play hooky from your "shoulds."

Lord, forgive me for ignoring Your example. Forgive me for trying to be a superhero and do it all. Our job is to care for others, just as Yours was. That doesn't mean that we don't care for ourselves. Show me, through Your Holy Spirit, to recognize those moments of white space where I can squeeze in some self-care. Give me courage to put myself first sometimes. Amen.

Where did Patient Care Go?

QUICK VERSE FOR THE nurses' lounge: "Jesus, knowing that the Father had given all things into his hands... rose from supper. He laid aside his outer garments, and taking a towel, tied it around his waist. Then he poured water into a basin and began to wash the disciples' feet and to wipe them with the towel that was wrapped around him." John 13:3-5

For further study later: John 13

It was eight o'clock, an hour past going-home time. I'd found a quiet room to chart. My keystrokes on the computer were getting more forceful. If I could've charted in all caps I would have!

Our unit had just switched software. It was completely different from the previous charting software. The hospital even had to put in new computers for it.

So, here I was, tapping away, having to double-check my work, backing up and starting over, clicking through different screens to find the right flowsheet or narrative notepad.

The previous weeks had been full of educational "opportunities" to learn it all, but it just wasn't the same as going live, especially when you work in an environment where "if it isn't charted, it isn't done." It was enough to make this girl use language her mama wouldn't approve of!

The worst part was that my patient today had a fetal demise. She was 22 weeks along and devastated. I had scribbled a few notes to myself on paper towels and kept up with vital signs reasonably well. Now I was piecing it all together.

But I was mad. What does it say about health-CARE if we don't have time to take care of our patients? We are busier babysitting computer screens than giving patients the attention they need!

It felt like a constant struggle between guilt over not being fully available for my patients and, later, the wakeful panic in the middle of the night, thinking I had forgotten to turn in that required paperwork for the c/section "time-out."

Putting my head in my hands, I whispered, "help me, please." I was hungry, tired, and mad. Who knew you could feel that much all in one moment?

Lord, You must be my supernatural grace right here, right now. I just want to get up and leave this mess. It isn't right that our patients suffer for the sake of bureaucracy and government watchdogs. Help me to focus so I can get home and rest. Give me courage to come back tomorrow. Let this system make sense quickly so I can move past this learning curve. And if my manager says one thing about me staying over tonight, I – I... Well, you'd better help me control my tongue, because I know exactly what I'll say to her, and it won't be pretty! Bless that sweet grieving family tonight. Give them comfort and peace during this tragedy. Amen

Terrible, No Good, Very Bad Christian

QUICK VERSE FOR THE nurses' lounge: "And we all, who with unveiled aces the Lord's glory, are being transformed into His ae with ever-increasing glory, which comes from the Lord, who is in the Spirit." 2 Corinthians 3:18 (New International Version)

For further study later: Ephesians 4:17-32

Let's face it - some days I stink as a disciple of Jesus. If He wanted to choose a kind, gentle, patient ambassador to show what He can do and be in a human being, He wasn't clearly thinking the day He chose me.

And when it comes to being a Christian nurse, well...Of course, I suppose you could substitute wife, mom, grocery shopper, human being, whatever for nurse on any given day. I get it. Jesus loves me; this I know. If I were the only human being on earth, He still would've died for me. Sometimes I just don't think I deserve it. The days when not only do I not enjoy my patients, but I also dislike them. The days when I would rather stay seated on my rear and finish charting than help my nurse friend clean up after her patient who just barfed all over herself for the third time today. The days I force myself not to make faces at the cranky doctor's back as he walks away, after a thoroughly humiliating dress-down at the nurses' station in front of everyone. The evening when I skip the staff meeting scheduled on my day off because I am "sick," or the way I grab the call schedule first so I can fill in all the "good" shifts before anyone else...

I mean, what kind of Christian does that?!

Oh, yeah, the being-transformed-into-His-image kind. More slowly some days than others, but nonetheless, changing.

And on this side of Pentecost, empowered by the Holy Spirit to "decide and do" His will (Philippians 2:13).

Most days I think my coworkers would say I am a good representative of who a Christ follower should be. The bad days are fewer and farther between - thank You, Jesus! The very fact that I regret my lousy attitude is evidence of how He is molding me into His image.

Jesus, thank You for loving me unconditionally. Thank You for putting Your Holy Spirit deep within me and reminding me, through Your Word, that You would gladly leave the ninety-nine sheltered sheep to find me, the little lost one. I pray for more nudges from You in those moments when I want to act like the old, fallen-human-nature-me. Thank You for the loving reminder that the former me is no longer who I am anymore.

Give me Your divine power to overcome the human impulse to behave in ways that aren't honoring to You. To quickly ask for forgiveness from You and from those I have hurt when I fail. I don't deserve Your grace, but I am eternally grateful for it. Amen.

Another Staff Meeting Day?

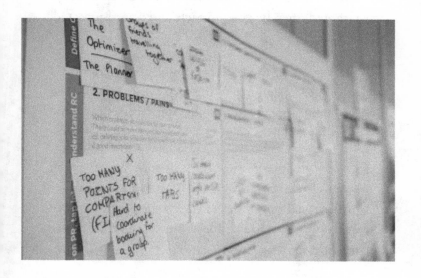

Quick Verse for the nurses' lounge: "And a young man named Eutychus, sitting at the window, sank into a deep sleep as Paul talked still longer. And being overcome by sleep, he fell down from the third story and was taken up dead." Acts 20:9

For Further Study Later: Galatians 5:22-26

Can't you see the followers of Jesus in heaven, talking about when they first became Christians? Like Eutychus, admitting he fell out of a window and died when Paul just wouldn't shut up already? Granted, then he got a miracle and was resurrected, but still...

I feel like that on staff meeting day, to be honest. I can't even imagine how the night shift feels! I need to remember my fruit of the Spirit verses on those days, for real.

Love - I do love most of these people. We have each other's backs, cover for each other in a way no other professional can understand. If Julie asks one more question, though, I'm gonna smack the back of her head. I wanna go home!

Joy - "Remember the first things" - isn't that in the Bible somewhere? I used to love to come to work each day, staff meeting or not. Today I struggle to sit here for an hour!

Peace - deep, cleansing breath as we are told they are adding *another step* in the process for retrieving blood from the blood bank. The patient will be dead by the time we go through it all! *It will be fine.*

Patience - as the nurse manager reads from her agenda. Can we read it ourselves and get back to you with questions we have? Okay, I get it. That adds to your busy workday.

Kindness - as Deena tells us about her reasons for not being able to take as much call as everyone else. We *all* have stuff, okay? Oh, yes, her mom has cancer, and she is being the caregiver on her days off. (Add her to my prayer list.)

Goodness - I love belonging to a company that gives back. For all the rules, it's great to belong to an organization that puts feet to their mission statement. Sign me up for the March of Dimes 5k

Gentleness - This one is easy today. Losing that patient yesterday has everyone upset, but especially Gretchen, her nurse. No one expects to lose a 29-year-old, healthy mother of two. Lord, give me the words to remind Gretchen that nothing can be done about an amniotic embolus - it wasn't anyone's fault.

Faithfulness - I don't know if it is the work we do or the things we see, but many of us recognize our need for the Lord. I feel blessed to work with many men and women of faith.

Self-control - It's come full circle today. I'm feeling overwhelmed and teary as I realize that, despite the difficulties, I really do love this job, these people, and how we all rock at getting it all done.

Thank You, Lord, for a better attitude now. Amen.

Mama Said There'd be Days Like This

QUICK VERSE FOR THE nurses' lounge: "I lift up my eyes to the hills.

From where does my help come? My help comes from the Lord, who made heaven and earth." Psalm 121:1-2

Further study for later: Psalms 121

"Abby died just now," the charge nurse informed me as I stepped onto the unit.

We had been expecting it, but it hit me hard.

Abby was special. Her blue eyes could light up the place the minute she walked in. She was adorable and silly. Yet she was like the "very bad" girl of the nursery rhyme when she didn't get her way. The place resounded with her screams when she was mad.

Also, she was young. Just four years old – way younger to die than the average life expectancy for cystic fibrosis patients in. At that time, they generally lived into their late twenties/early thirties.

Most significant to me, it was the first time I had been faced with a death. I had worked here for months, but my patients were doing well. They came in, got their "cleanout," and went home. Some of the older teens were in further stages of the disease, but no one I had cared for was in end-stage CF.

I put my bag in my locker and went out to the nurses' station.

The scene there was heartbreaking. Nurses with red-rimmed eyes were huddled there. Abby's doctor consoled her parents near her room.

"Jennifer, I know it's hard, but can you go in with Tracy and do the end-of-life care? She'll show you what needs to be done, but the rest of us–" She waved at the other nurses, her voice breaking.

I could be more objective - right?

The room was quiet as we entered. My heart was pounding as I neared the bed.

Abby's eyes were closed, her arms by her side. The grayish-blue tinge of her face and the stillness of her chest were the only evidence she wasn't alive.

As Tracy walked me through the steps to care for someone who has died – take out tubes, bathe her, comb her hair – I sensed the Lord's presence almost physically. He comforted me as I performed the tasks.

"She's not here any longer. No more is she in pain, struggling for every breath. You can do this. I've promised, as the Holy Spirit, to give you strength for hard things."

As I gently washed her tiny arms and legs, I spoke quietly to the Lord, as well.

Lord, comfort Abby's family right now. Thank You for being near to the brokenhearted. Everyone is sad over this little girl's death- she is gone too soon. I don't understand why You allow this disease, but I know that You're good. Show Your goodness to us all today, in big and small ways. Thank You for staying right by my side through this first sorrow of my career. May I be Your hands and feet, even voice, to this grieving family. Amen.

No Friends Like Nurse Friends

QUICK VERSE FOR NURSES' lounge: A friend is always loyal, and a brother is born to help in time of need." Proverbs 17:17 New Living Translation

Further study for later: 1 Samuel 20

I don't know about you, but some days I feel like I am fighting in the trenches. The call lights never stop, the patients' families are all unhappy, the doctors want those test results yesterday, and there isn't enough time to get all the patient care done.

Not to downplay what actual soldiers go through in a war (some of you have been there, done that!), but I'm sure you get where I'm coming from.

The upside is that you bond on those days like you could never do in less time-sensitive professions. When someone's life is at stake in the ER based on how well you all work together, when you're racing a patient to the OR for an emergency surgery, when the answers aren't coming and the whole healthcare team is putting their heads together to figure out the next step in a patient's care, when every available RN shows up to help when your patient tanks – yeah, that's the cement that binds you for life.

I remember days when we had women laboring in the hallway behind a screen (yeah, the old-fashioned kind with white fabric and steel) because the unit was so full there wasn't another place for them. Talk about no room at the inn!

You do what you can in those times. You watch out for each other's patients, you help with tasks when you can, you high-five in the hall, and cry in the bathroom when you get thirty seconds. And you pray that the next shift is on time!

Thank You for nurse friends that are totally tracking with me when I'm so excited that I made it through a shift with no one coding, or puking on me, or threatening to sue. That laugh at the same things - my googly eyes over that guy's hot "rope veins" at the party, or the nurse memes that no one else gets, or the hilarious story about cleaning up a patient's BM only to roll them back onto the clean bed, then having to clean it all over again. I'm grateful for friends that will stand nearby when I go in the isolation room so they can bring things I inevitably forgot. Friends I can swap gross stories with over a plate of Mexican food. Friends that commiserate when I get stuck with three out of four weekend shifts. I'm grateful for friends who hand me the tissues and cover my patients for twenty minutes while I cry in the bathroom because my favorite patient died last night. Friends who don't get their feelings hurt when I say "no way" to dinner after work – all I want to do is go shower and put on pajamas at home. Friends who swap shifts so I can attend my son's play or my spouse's softball game. And it's even better when your best buds are all on your shift at once! Amen.

I Get to Do This!

QUICK VERSE FOR THE nurses' lounge: "This service
that you perform is not only supplying the needs of the
Lord's people but is also overflowing in many expressions of
thanks to God." 2 Cor. 9:12 (New International Version)

For further study later: 1 Thess. 4:9-12

Today is one of those days that I am full of gratitude for this career I have chosen. I'm a simple girl when it comes to work. I don't need a fancy office or a big title. Most days I am just grateful for the little things.

Things like:

- Four consecutive days off in a row (how did that happen?)

- Working a shift with all my favorite people

- When my patient falls asleep with their medication barcode facing up

- When we make it through a full moon night without a stat anything,

no crazies, and a low-key shift

- When that grouchy hospitalist isn't on

- When the night shift gets here early, and report goes quick

- When I get the "difficult" IV stick on the first try

- When the clodhopper nursing shoes I bought for $120 (on sale!) are comfortable for the whole shift

- When I get called off for the holiday shift because the census is low

- When my day is full of hilarity, like the guy who's covered in tattoos almost, but not quite, passes out from a needle stick; or the baby is delivered with the IUD in her chubby little hand; or the sweet little old lady has a mouth like a sailor (sorry, Lord, but it's kinda funny!)

- When I have a good attitude about my job, rather than a bad one

Because doesn't the day go better when we look at things as blessings instead of curses? When we seek out the treasures rather than moan about the drudgery? We truly, really, honestly love this job or we wouldn't have stuck with it as long as we have. We get to be a part of the Great Physician's work - healing, helping, opening the door for miracles, or ushering folks into eternity.

God, these are the things that remind me that You love to give good gifts to Your children. A full day of these don't come along often, but it is the sprinkling of grace-dust throughout the weeks that bring joy to this nurse heart. That keep me sane when I think I can't go one more day in this exhausting field. The truth is, I love this profession you have given me, but it is nice to be reminded why occasionally. Thank You, Lord! Amen.

Adrenaline Rush

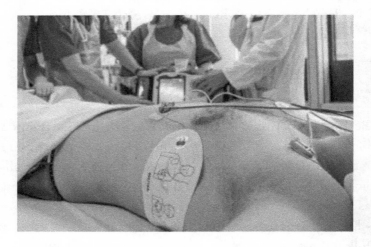

QUICK VERSE FOR THE nurses' lounge: "So Thomas, called the Twin, said to his fellow disciples, "Let us also go, that we may die with him." John 11:16

Further study for later: John 11:1-16, John 20:19-31

Nurses all have various levels of excitement tolerance in their jobs. Rehab nurses have tough moments, but I'm not sure what heart-pounding anxiety they feel. A trauma ED nurse daily has more adrenaline rushes than I care to have in my lifetime!

I'm not sure I would want some of the jobs I had as a younger nurse again.

Not because of the physicality of the job, or the mental strain, but because I'm ready to settle into an easier pace of life, with each day bringing routine.

I chuckle now, though I was irritated then, at a moment of terror that was too much for me. I'd gone in to check a patient's cervix. The baby's heart rate showed signs of dipping during contractions. As it was her second baby, I knew labor could progress quickly.

Immediately, as I palpated her cervix, I knew something wasn't right. There was an odd bump and a buzzing sensation under my fingers (yes, L&D nurses, you know what I was feeling). Instead of doing all the things my training taught me, I snatched my hand out and whirled to face my supervisor, who, providentially, walked in to see what was going on.

"Uh, I'm not sure what I'm feeling," I told her.

She came up behind me and, you guessed it, upon exam found a prolapsed cord. Unlike me, she stayed there, pushing the baby's head off the cervix while I slammed the emergency light and put the patient's head down. Nurses poured in. They helped increase IV rates for anesthesia and place oxygen while I called the CRNA and OB to inform them of the necessary stat c-section.

In the meantime, my face stained with embarrassment, I was ashamed that it was my preceptor keeping the baby's head off the umbilical cord, rather than me. (If you think OB nurses are kind, empathetic creatures, you would be wrong. They teased me unmercifully for a while, until someone else's oopsie turned their attention elsewhere.)

We always think of Peter as Mr. Cocky, yet he was not the only disciple with attitude problems. Thomas was ready to die for Jesus if anyone in Jerusalem messed with him. Yet he disappeared, too, after the crucifixion. He did not even hang with them in the locked room, hidden away. He found his own spot, so he was not there when Jesus appeared to all of them that first time. James and John – along with their mother – fought over who was to be first in Jesus' eyes.

Funny how we think, in the hypothetical, we will be superheroes until the rubber meets the road. When it gets scary, how do we respond?

Fortunately, I redeemed myself through the years, handling other emergencies well. I even enjoyed the moments of excitement when we pushed ourselves to get a baby out quickly to avoid bad outcomes.

Lord, remind me that Your grace is sufficient in my weakness. Give me patience and competence in moments that push me beyond what I think I can manage. Amen.

Just Another Manic Monday

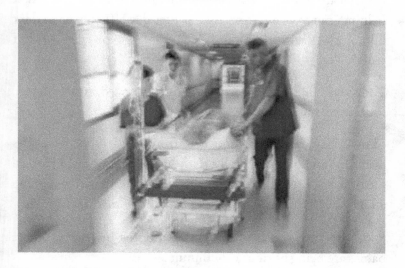

QUICK VERSE FOR THE nurses' lounge: "Honor her for all that her hands have done, and let her works bring her praise at the city gate." Proverbs 31:31 (New International Version)

For Further Study Later: 2 Corinthians 12:1-10

Some days I wonder how we make it through the day. Our jobs can be insane - not just the physical side, but the emotional one, as well.

Most of us are good at helping one another out - pitching in when one assignment is hard and another is easier, covering for one another so we can grab a quick bite to eat, helping to turn/clean/transport patients. (Some nurses aren't so good at helping, but that is a story for another day.) Then we use dark humor to survive the draining emotions involved - sad, but true.

Today was one of "those" days. I'm bone-tired, to be honest. So.Many.Babies.

I know they are precious and a gift from You. Yes, yes, my job is beautiful and joyful and all the things people want to remind me of when I tell them what I do. Yet I want to run screaming after a day like today when I see pregnant women at the mall!

I wonder what was happening nine months ago that all these babies are being born now? Hmmm...

I'm so thankful I made it through this shift. At one point, when I got that next assignment, I had to fight not to cry. Ain't nobody got time to cry today!

My feet hurt, my back hurts, I'm hungry, and I got to pee once in twelve hours. Good thing we don't get to drink much on these days, or the situation would be dire. That doctor is so #blessed I didn't bite his head off when he followed me DOWN THE HALL TO THE BATHROOM to ask about his patient's lab results! Look it up yourself! (If I weren't trying to be more Christ-like, I might have used language that isn't "helpful for building others up"!)

Somehow, I finished that crazy run of three twelve-hour shifts. And managed not to kill anyone. Although it was nutso busy, it was all routine. No crash c/sections or seizing patients or neonatal resuscitations. I don't think I could've managed a stat run to the OR!

*Lord, sorry for my sarcasm, profane internal words, and ingratitude. I **do** have a beautiful job and, most days, I'm grateful. I wouldn't have minded one easy shift this week. Please, I'm asking for the rush to be over when I go back to work in two days? And now, may I make the most of my days off. Prayers for an understanding spouse when I fall asleep at 8 tonight during the movie! Amen.*

Not the Boss of Me (oh, wait...)

QUICK VERSE FOR THE nurses' lounge: "Let every person be subject to the governing authorities. For there is no authority except from God, and those that exist have been instituted by God." Romans 13:1

For further study later: Romans 13:1-7

I didn't realize until I started full-time in the hospital my issue with authority. I had been the "good girl" growing up, compliant.

It was a different world in nursing. Once I got my feet under me and knew what I was doing, I didn't like being told how to do things.

If there's one thing healthcare in the twenty-first century is, it's this – you'd better do what you're told, when you're told, how you're told. The big corporations that run hospitals and medical institutions don't tolerate straying from policy and procedure, even if sometimes they don't make practical sense.

That's what would kill me – the nitpicking over tiny details when people's health was at stake. It's like the nursing meme that asks sarcastically "but did you die?" No.

Did you get better? Was the desired outcome achieved?

You see where my mind was. It came out – in my attitude, my words, and my tendency to do things my own way. Unfortunately, you can only get away with it so long.

Today I was complaining to the Lord about a reprimand from my boss.

"That's stupid. What is up with micromanaging such a tiny detail? Of course, I'm going to resist it! We as nurses must stand up for ourselves in this environment. Yada yada..."

Sometimes the Lord is gentle with me. Today He was not.

It doesn't matter how you feel about it. Those are the rules. You *need to suck it up and deal with the fact that I have placed this* *person in authority for a reason. Those laws are there for a purpose* *and it might just be to save your butt from bigger mistakes.* (Yes, sometimes God says butt, at least to hard-headed me.) *Until the* *rules change, if they don't go against My Law, you need to comply.*

It took missteps and do-overs, but I did learn to go along to get along most of the time. I will always struggle with it to an extent, but I learned to bite my tongue, see the other point of view, and become more teachable.

Maybe you're there too. There are lots of checks and balances in healthcare. Sometimes the burden of them becomes overwhelming. No doubt there are things we need to speak against, especially when finances are elevated above patient care.

But are there things you are complaining about simply because you don't like them? Because they seem dumb? Maybe you can let them go. For the sake of a positive workplace. For the sake of learning to treat even your boss how you would want to be treated if the situation were reversed. For the sake of following orders of The Boss of us all.

Lord, you know this area is a struggle for me. When I don't understand the rationale, it's hard for me not to question. You are gonna need to help me out here. Please give me the fruit of the Spirit of self-control. Amen.

Needing the Great Physician, Myself

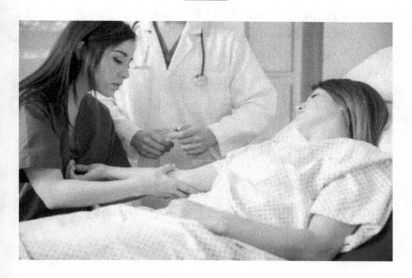

QUICK VERSE FOR THE nurses' lounge: "Jesus said to them, 'I suppose you'll quote me the proverb, 'Doctor, go and heal yourself before you try to heal others.' And you'll say, 'Work the miracles here in your hometown that we heard you did in Capernaum.'" Luke 4:23 (New International Version)

For Further study later: Romans 2:13-24

I'm not supposed to be sick! I'm the caregiver and the healer. I don't do so well staying in bed - or obeying doctor's orders! I don't want other people taking care of me (for one thing, they just can't do it like I can.)

And what about work? These days, we only get so many sick days. Am I *really* contagious? Am I *sure* I can't make it through a twelve-hour shift?

Some days the Lord Almighty Himself has set aside for rest - the Sabbath, for example. Other days we have set aside to take time off - like vacations. They aren't always restful, but we can pretend.

Other days, God forces us to stop and rest.

I don't think any nurses are good at rest. Even when we are sick, we toss a load of laundry in, or start the dishwasher, or...

The problem is, if we don't care for ourselves when we are a little sick, we can get Capital S Sick. Bronchitis turns into pneumonia. The flu turns into sepsis.

Or, more serious, the stage 1 breast cancer turns into stage 4.

Let's listen to our nagging voice inside -the Holy Spirit. When was the last time you had a physical? A mammogram? Are you taking your statin, your baby aspirin, your Vitamin D?

Yep, I'm going there. Nag, nag. Find some exercise you love– tennis, dancing, hiking, swimming. Include the kiddos if you have little ones at home.

Eat a few vegetables occasionally. You and your friend or spouse or S.O. take a cooking class - you might find you enjoy it!

I say this because I've heard from the Lord that it is my turn to care for myself. I don't have excuses anymore. My kids are grown and almost grown. Even though I'm busy, I have time to spend on healthy diet choices and exercise.

Let's face it — we don't take care of ourselves because we don't value ourselves. It's the nurse curse - the worst patients, the least compliant people in the doctor's office, the last to practice self-care.

Jesus, you know this staying in bed thing is hard for me. Give me your supernatural patience. Remind me that I am worth it - the child of a King! Step in and knock me flat, if you must, before I get too ill. Protect me from my own poor choices - though I don't deserve it! I love your care for me. Amen.

Work-Life Balance in Luke's Gospel

QUICK VERSE FOR THE Nurses' Lounge: "Yet the news about Him spread all the more, so that crowds of people came to hear him and to be healed of their sicknesses. But Jesus often withdrew to lonely places and prayed." Luke 5:15-16 (New International Version)

For Further study later: Verses in Luke below

Nursing is a tough gig. We see hard things - pain, sickness, death, trauma, financial hardships, and family stress.

We face an imperfect healthcare environment. The politics and drama involved can be enough for us to wish we'd been a bus driver! We may try to alleviate it by changing jobs, but it follows us. Although we act like a professional, it eventually affects us. We bring it home in exhaustion, stress, and impatience. It spills into our home life, health, and relationships with others.

There is One who modeled the perfect work-life balance - Jesus. He

considered his "work" a joy. This was most exemplified in the gospel that presented Jesus in His humanity, written by a physician, Luke.

We can learn how to balance caring for others and caring for ourselves from Jesus. He had a job to do, but He never let it interfere with His relationships.

How did He do it?

1) Acknowledged God is in control. Luke 12:25-26 - "Who of you by worrying can add a hour to your life? Since you cannot do this very little thing, do not worry about the rest."

2) Had a healthy lifestyle - nutrition, rest, relationships. Luke 6:1-5 - "One Sabbath Jesus was going through the grainfields, and his disciples began to pick some heads of grain... and eat the kernels. Some of the Pharisees asked, "Why are you doing what is unlawful on the Sabbath?"

3) Jesus answered them, "Have you never read what David did when he and his companions were hungry? He entered the house of God, and taking the consecrated bread, he ate what is lawful only for priests to eat."

4) Focused on caring only for those He was *called* to help. Luke 9: 20-22 - "A woman who had been subject to bleeding for twelve years came up behind him and touched the edge of his cloak. She said to herself, "If I only touch his cloak, I will be healed." Jesus turned and saw her. "Take heart, daughter," he said, "your faith has healed you." And the woman was healed at that moment.

5) 7) And the list goes on...

Lord, teach us how to balance our love and care for others with our need to leave some for our family. Order our days that we can be at our best for all You have called us to serve. Amen.

My Weird Love Affair

QUICK VERSE FOR THE nurses' lounge: "Have regard to the prayer of your servant...that your eyes may be open night and day to this house, the place of which you have said, 'My name shall be there,' that You may listen to the prayer that your servant offers towards this place." 1 Kings 8: 28-29

For Further Study later: 1 Kings 8:22-26

I love hospitals. I'm probably not supposed to admit that. People are sick, getting unwelcome news, or even dying there. I've spent a good part of my life there, day in and day out. Aren't I over that yet?

Not yet! Since I was a "candy striper," I've been fascinated with hospitals.

Shiny, brand-new ones. Faded old ones. I'm not sure what that says about me.

Maybe it says that was where God called me. My love for those big, bright, bustling buildings confirmed that calling.

The smells of antiseptic, the overhead pages, the people of all shapes, sizes, and colors hurrying around. The whirring and buzzing of machines and the low murmur of voices.

I've been proud to be a part of that environment. Glad to wear the RN badge. I don't even mind when friends ask me to identify a strange rash!

Unlike some of my friends, I liked nursing school. Not every class - pharmacology killed me! - but I enjoyed learning, practicing, clinicals, and cramming. I don't want to go back for more, mind you, but I enjoyed the first time around.

I didn't like being the "new kid," unsure of myself - perfectionist tendencies! but I enjoyed the freedom of finally being on my own, without a preceptor. I did not mind BEING the preceptor, years later, and I got used to being the charge nurse, even later, as scary as that was.

I liked changing units - going from peds to post-surgical to labor and delivery. Different roles don't bother me - OR nurse, labor nurse, recovery nurse. If I wasn't in charge of patient care in an unfamiliar area, I didn't even mind taking my turn on a different floor - playing tech in ER, CNA on postpartum.

The hardest transition was leaving the hospital. It is amazing how much of our identity gets wrapped up in our job, even if we think it will never happen. Especially when you have a love affair with hospitals.

I won't go back to working in that setting. It is a hard job - physically, emotionally, even spiritually. But I know that I am in the center of God's will for me - caring for others in whatever setting He places me in.

Did *you* feel God calling you to where you work? Do you feel God calling you somewhere else? It is easy for us to go about our days and ignore the still, small voice inside telling us what's next.

Lord, thank You for those years walking the halls of the hospital and all that meant - even the hard days. You call each of us to our places "for such a time as this." Remind me to listen to Your voice, to respond to Your call. Wherever that may be. Amen.

Nothing We Did

QUICK VERSE FOR THE nurses' lounge: "Confess your sins to each other and pray for each other so that you may be healed. The earnest prayer of a righteous person has great power and produces wonderful results." James 5:16 (New International Version)

For further study later: Mark 2:1-13

The Lord showed up today in a big way! How often I believe the lie that miracles were for "back then." I see so many in my job daily, I'm sure, but it is easy for me to dismiss them as the marvels of modern-day medicine.

Or coincidence, or genetics. Or a million other things.

But today there was no doubt, for any of us, from Prayer Warrior Wilma to Atheist Dr. Lewis. There was no human way that patient could have responded to his treatment. We were ready to have the organ donation talk, but her husband would not give up yet. He rallied around his praying friends and family, and they stormed heaven and God came through!

I feel overwhelmed in these moments - when I get to witness the Great

Physician step in and heal the thing in ways that no other world-renowned surgeon or specialist ever could. It is an in-your-face reminder that Yahweh alone is sovereign and can do whatever He wants.

I know that He has gifted me and other healthcare workers with the healing touch. Some days, though, we are like the friends who brought the lame man on the mat to Jesus through the roof in Luke 5. We just need to bring our patients to Jesus so we can watch Him do His thing.

Too often we are fearful of bringing prayer into our work in the hospital

rooms and exam rooms and surgical suites.

I'm trying to be brave and intentional about this. In those times when I have asked a patient if they would like me to pray with them, they have been receptive. Even if they say no, it is not as though people are so offended that they complain to a supervisor or ask for another nurse. Our world has become so fearful of bringing offense that we have forgotten that we have the greatest healing power at our call, 24/7 - the power of the Holy Spirit!

Lord, I praise You for those moments when You remind us that You alone have the power of life and death. Sometimes You use our talents to work healing, but some days it is all You. Forgive me for the times when I don't first bring the ailments and illnesses of my patients to You. Forgive me for taking it all for granted. Help me to remember to seek Your wisdom and Your cure before even stepping foot into my patient's room. May I always be in awe of how You work. Amen.

A Place of Healing or Harm?

———

QUICK VERSE FOR THE Nurses' Lounge: "But godliness with contentment is great gain, for we brought nothing into this world, and we cannot take anything out of the world." 1 Timothy 6:6-7

For further study later: 1 Timothy 6:3-8

How can this be real? That precious nurse is lying in a coma!

How is it possible that violence is sweeping through hospitals with such regularity now?

I heard about it on the news but could not wrap my mind around it. I had to call a friend who works there, too. No, it is not in a third world country. It is in a hospital right around the corner.

Pent-up rage is making monsters of many of us. Not just with guns by gangs, but us — out on the freeways, in boardrooms, in living rooms. Road rage, sexual assault, human trafficking, knife crime, violent spewing from keyboards. What have we become?

I have had a surgeon kicking at me until I left "his" OR, I have seen physicians throw a chart across the room, and instruments thrown by angry practitioners. The red-faced, shrieking orderly cussing out my manager at the nurses' station, the grieving father who threw a full cup of coffee down the hall — the only one I sympathized with. And yet, no matter the circumstances, it is terrifying. We wonder if it will spiral into destructiveness. We know sometimes it does.

I guess, naively, I am always surprised when it happens in a place where people are supposed to be mending, not being broken. Emotions are high.

Relationships are tested.

It is not only our bodies that need healing, but our souls, as well. Jesus came to give life abundantly - that means in body, soul, and spirit. The world needs a Savior, a Physician, to heal, strengthen, and counsel.

So, what do we do? How do we make a difference?

First, we need to **Pray**: Pray for a peaceful resolution to strife. Pray for wise words and a calming spirit. Pray for comfort and peace in heartbreaking situations.

Next, we need to **Prevent**: When we see emotions escalating, call security to have them be on alert. Separate angry parties. Speak softly. Educate.

Next, **Protect**: Activate the security protocol. Pull bystanders out of the line of fire. Follow protocols. Pull back from the angry party.

Lord, I ask that You go with me this shift. Bring peace where there is strife. Bring comfort where there is grief. Bring understanding where there is confusion. You are all-knowing and all-seeing. Give me some of Your wisdom today to diminish the heated emotions and anticipate problematic situations. Protect me as I go about my work. Amen.

People, Paperwork, & Patience - Plus One

QUICK VERSE FOR THE nurses' lounge: "Do not be anxious about anything, but in every situation, by prayer and petition, with thanksgiving, present your requests to God." Philippians 4:6

For further study later: Psalm 86

When I consider the most constant parts of healthcare – across all specialties and locations – there are three P's we can count on being an essential part of our day. Plus, one that we *need*.

People, paperwork, and patience.

So many people! Smart people, not-so-smart people, short, tall, fat, thin, healthy, sick, all shades of the neutral rainbow and of the political spectrum.

So much paperwork! Even if it is mostly on computer, it's paperwork. If you still must write longhand charting, God bless you.

So much patience required — mostly because of the previous two! Patience with patients - ha! Patience with their family and friends. Patience with colleagues, with management, with physicians, and with ancillary staff. Patience with ourselves, as we navigate our days.

Personally, I don't know how anyone gets through it all without the most important P - *prayer*.

Prayer does not come naturally. I believe that's why Jesus had to give the disciples a lesson on how to pray.

Some of you may call me irreverent, but I have amended The Lord's Prayer, to suit my nursing life.

> *Our Great Physician, which art in Heaven*
>
> *Blessed be Your Name*
>
> *Let wellness come or may Your Will be done*
>
> *Here in this place as it is in heaven*
>
> *Give me this day a break for lunch*

Forgive me for my murderous thoughts towards others,
As I am sure they must forgive me.

Lead me not into temptation to make up a respiratory
rate when I

Have multiple vitals to take but deliver me from my
tendency to make stuff up.

For Thine is the Kingdom, and the Healing Power,
and the Glory forever.

Amen.

Seriously, though, prayer is a vital ingredient when we work in the healing professions.

Sometimes we only have time for breath prayers. You know the one —

"Jesus, help!"

Sometimes they are a desperate plea. "*I cannot make it through this day without You. I feel overwhelmed and hungry. Please supernaturally intervene so I remember all I need to do and get it done before the doctor comes for rounds. This med is new to me - remind me how to give it again? God, Nelda Nurse is on my last nerve again. I need Your divine kindness with her. Amen.*"

Most days they occur at the beginning of the day. "*Wow, all my patients have crazy acuity levels. Help me not to kill them,*" or

At the end of the day *"Did I remember everything? Can you quicken this brain of mine so I can recall what I need to complete before report? I just have thirty more minutes of this shift - keep me going, Lord."*

The tough ones are the prayers that wake us up off-shift. *"Lord, bring healing to that kind man. I pray that You give him more years with his family." "Jesus, did I ever take that poor girl her extra blanket." "Ugh, what else did I forget? Help me to rest now, please. Amen.*

Legacy of Caring

QUICK VERSE FOR THE nurses' lounge: "Know therefore that the Lord your God is God, the faithful God who keeps covenant and steadfast love with those who love Him and keep His commandments, to a thousand generations." Deuteronomy 7:9

For Further study later: 1 Chronicles 16:8-36

Many healthcare professionals have a long line of family before them who also are "in the field." Is it a personality type? Like there are generations of teachers and police officers?

I don't have the research, but it makes sense. Not only do we pass on physical genetic traits, like blue eyes or dimples, but we also pass on emotional ones. Nurses are typically compassionate, giving, and at least moderately self-sacrificing. I know there are days, weeks even, when you *just.can't.* - but go with me here...

If we weren't at least some of the above, would we get up before the sun — or get home as the sun rises? Would we go a whole shift without eating so we can make sure our patients are properly cared for? Would we smile and say "No worries — I'm used to it" when our patient apologizes over and over for the diarrhea she has?

My grandma wanted to be a nurse, but she was not able, due to circumstances, to graduate from high school. My mother is a nurse – she has worked in an ICU in a Los Angeles County Hospital, in a rehab unit, and then in hospice by the time I began obstetric nursing. (We would joke that I brought 'em in and she took 'em out. Yeah, that's disrespectful, I know, but y'all are nurses. You get dark humor.)

My eldest wanted to be a doctor, but decided his personality fits his daddy's former profession of marketing better. My middle one has the personality for medicine, but no desire to go there. And my youngest wants to be the engineer. He will be the most hilarious engineer anyone has ever met. So, I guess the medical gene stopped with me.

The Word says we are all made in the image of God. That is something isn't it? Once we receive His life, we take on His characteristics — genetic traits, if you will. All that He is can be ours - empowered by the filling of the Holy Spirit.

Since God is God — omniscient, omnipresent, and omnipotent – He can be what anyone needs in any situation. You need a mother's tenderness? You need a father's patience? You need a potter's ability to make beauty out of a lump of clay? You need a farmer's wisdom as to when to sow or when to reap? He has all of these and more.

Thank You, Abba, for making us all unique and yet like You. Thank You that, in those moments we can't naturally be gentle, we can't naturally be kind — we have Your divine life within us so that can. Remind us to turn to You when we are lacking. Remind us that our patients are also made in your image, whether they know it or not, and to treat them with the kindness and sympathy everyone deserves. Amen.

Ethical Dilemmas

QUICK VERSE FOR THE nurses' lounge: "...our God whom we serve is able to deliver us from the burning fiery furnace, and He will deliver us out of your hand, O king. But if not, be it known to you, O king, that we will not serve your gods or worship the golden image that you have set up." Daniel 3: 17-18

For further study later: Daniel 3

"It's okay, Maria. You can go be with your daughter. I'm here — I can take care of Mom for now."

My mother smiled and patted the caregiver's arm. She had come to stay with my grandmother for a couple of weeks, aware that she was nearing the end.

During those two weeks, Mom cared tenderly for her, making sure she changed position every two hours and bathed her regularly — just as she was trained in nursing school. She administered her blood pressure pills and gave her the required insulin.

Also, every morning she propped her up in bed and gave her coffee with cream (lukewarm now, with a straw) and a Danish. Mom didn't make her walk around the living room twice a day if she wasn't up for it. If

Grandmother wanted to eat lunch and watch her "stories" (otherwise known as soap operas) in bed, that is what she did. The two of them looked through old photos and laughed and cried.

It made her death that much sweeter to Mom, months later.

"For just a bit, I got my mother back. Sure, she had her moments of confusion, and it broke my heart to hear her crying 'Take me, Jesus' in the nighttime hours. But I got to give her the tender loving care she had given me all those years."

Some might say that that was irresponsible of my mom, to allow her to eat foods not on the diabetic diet and to cave when she didn't want to get some exercise. To my mom, it was an easy decision. Her eighty-nine-year- old mother, nearing the end of her life, was going to enjoy her visit with her daughter for the last time. So what if the cream cheese Danish shortened her life by eight hours? She was ready to go.

Some dilemmas are not so easy. With all our wonderful advances in medicine, it brings up harder questions. Do we keep pushing for lifesaving measures on younger and younger preemies, even if we know their quality of life will be affected? Do we "help" the elderly or infirm die sooner? Do we transplant a new liver into the man who is a recovering alcoholic? Are we afraid to admit we will not assist with an elective termination of pregnancy?

At some point in our career, we will be faced with a decision to do something that goes against what we know to be right. In most states, you can simply ask to be excused from their care, for reasons of conscience. But what if you can't? Have you thought it through? Do you have a plan, like the emergency plan we are *supposed* to have in place in case of a house fire? Are you willing, like Shadrach, Meshach, and Abednego to stand up for what you believe even if it means humiliation or job loss?

Lord, make me brave to do Your will, no matter what the cost. Give me the courage of Steven who looked up into heaven as he was stoned and saw You standing at the throne of God, ready to receive him. No compromise, no fear. Amen.

In a Crisis

QUICK VERSE FOR THE Nurses' Lounge: "Casting all your anxieties on him, because he cares for you." 1 Peter 5:7

For further study later: 1 Peter 5

As I type this, the world is experiencing a whole new thing - Covid-19. The transmission rate is scary, the unusual ways it manifests don't make sense. Some don't even know they've been infected because their symptoms mimic a cold. Some go into respiratory distress and need to be ventilated.

It is affecting the world of healthcare in various ways. Some practitioners are not working (no elective surgeries); some are working overtime. Some places have all the PPE they need; some are reusing the same masks over and over.

Amid this is the fear. The viral load those on the frontlines are exposed to is high. "Am I going to get sick? Will I bring it home to my family?" "Can I keep working these crazy hours?"

The job we have can affect us in frightening ways. Whether it is disease or even danger (I know so many nurses who have been physically or verbally assaulted), where do we get the strength to show up again and again? We never imagined this in nursing school!

Healthcare workers are being hailed as heroes. Yet, we think, what are our options? Not show up? When we were saving lives before, where were the accolades? If we are such heroes, how come the administration and healthcare executives still want to put dollars over safety?

There are no easy answers. In a time of crisis, whether it is after a patient dies that you thought you could save, or after you've been stuck by a used needle, or when you are going into the isolation unit of a desperately ill patient, we have to decide. Is this worth it? Do I love this enough to put myself (and even my family, when there is infectious disease involved) at risk day after day?

John 15:13 says, "Greater love has no one than this: to lay down his life for his friends."

What about for strangers? How much are you willing to sacrifice for a paycheck? And is that what this job is to you, a paycheck? Or is it a calling, a mission?

These are all questions we need to resolve in our own minds, our own lives. Times like these require getting real with the Lord. To seek His wisdom, His strength, and His purpose.

C.S. Lewis wrote "Pain insists on being attended to. God whispers to us in our pleasures, speaks in our consciences, but shouts in our pains. It is His megaphone to rouse a deaf world."

It is in our tough times that we learn to surrender to Him.

Lord, You know how nervous I am when I walk through those doors some days. It is not always life and death situations for only my patients, but even for me! Give me protection each day - from disease, from disaster, from danger. May I be a blessing to those I care for, and may I see how they bless me, as well. Amen.

A Different Kind of Diversity Training

QUICK VERSE FOR THE Nurses' Lounge: "Yes, I try to find common ground with everyone, doing everything I can to save some. I do everything to spread the Good News and share in its blessings." 1 Cor. 9:22b-23 (New Living Testament)

For further study later: 1 Corinthians 9

The room is dark. It smells faintly of - something - I can't quite identify. The room is full of women, sprawled on chairs and loungers. My patient tenses and pulls up her bedding, then relaxes when she sees that it is a female entering her room.

"Good morning," I whisper, as I slide the blood pressure cuff up her arm. "How are you feeling?"

She smiles and nods, her head bouncing a few times.

"Would you like some pain medicine?" I ask, trying to be clearer in my intention for the question this time.

"Oh, yes!" Her eyes turn up with her smile this time, relief flooding her eyes.

It has been a knowledge that is slow in coming – learning the habits and cues and tendencies of other cultures. They view nursing, pain relief, childbirth, and many other aspects of healthcare differently than we do here in the US. I have not always,

I'm ashamed to say, been very patient with the different ways people react to hospitalization, pain, and disease. I also have struggled not to stereotype and assume that all people with a certain background or nationality will react in the same way!

The world has become very multi-cultural through the generations, thanks to air flight, technology, and communication advances. It is not only the United States that is a melting pot anymore.

Most healthcare settings do not lend themselves to overt sharing of one's faith, except for some religious institutions. We can always find ways to show our Christianity in what we wear, an offer to pray with the patient, if they desire, or pointing the way to the chapel (even secular institutions still have those!).

We must, like the apostle Paul, be sensitive to the different people we encounter daily, as Christian nurses. It requires vigilance, unselfishness, and patience, to give the "something extra." To reconsider our communication and our tactics. To "show" the love of Jesus even if we can't "tell" of it.

Lord, like St. Francis of Assisi, I pray that You will make me an "instrument of Your peace. Where there is despair, let me give hope. Where there is darkness, let me give light, where there is sadness let me give joy." Shine through me in what I do and say - to those I "get" and those I do not. May I be kind, patient, and sensitive to everyone You love and came to the earth to save. And, as opportunity presents, may I give a reason for the hope that is in me. Amen.

What is the Source of my Identity?

QUICK VERSE FOR THE Nurses' Lounge: Matthew 7:24—"Therefore everyone who hears these words of mine and puts them into practice is like a wise man who built his house on the rock." (New International Version)

For further study later: Matthew 7:24-28

After 25 years in nursing, I took a break after my oldest entered his senior year of high school. I wanted to spend as much time as I could with him before he left home.

It was a strange thing to not go into work every week. It was awkward to pause a moment when people asked what my occupation was. I had always said I was a homemaker, but I had always then added "But my for-money job is a nurse."

Even when I began volunteering as an RN at a pregnancy resources clinic, I still felt — what? Not a *real* nurse?

I finally decided I was depressed. It wasn't just that my son would soon be going off to college, though that was part of it. I had so identified as a nurse - even more specifically, as a Labor and Delivery nurse - that I felt like I had lost a big part of my identity.

I took a deep breath and told my family, my doctor, and then a compassionate Christian therapist what I was going through. After a few months of sessions (plus a few rounds of "happy pills" as we jokingly called them around the unit I used to work in), I began to recognize my troublesome attitude of identifying overly with the wrong "hat" in my life.

Although this is a devotional book by a nurse and for nurses, I believe we all first and foremost want to be identified as Christ followers. Whether in our workplaces, our churches, or our homes, we want others to see His love shining through our eyes. When our occupation is gone - through retirement or vocation switch or through injury — what rock do we stand on?

Lord, You know how I love my career as a nurse. I always want to be involved in some way with caring for others' health - mental, physical, or emotional. But I long to please You first. So do with me what You will. Send me where You want me to go. Prevent me from stepping outside of Your direction for my life. Let me be Your ambassador in whatever stage of life I am in. Thank you for people to come alongside me and remind me that my worth is not found in a career, or a position, or anything other than Your love and Your declaration over me that I am a child of the King. Amen.

Different Shift

QUICK VERSE FOR THE nurses' lounge: "I can do all things through Him who strengthens me." Philippians 4:13

Further study for later: Philippians 4:8-20

Okay, I can do this! Phew! I haven't done this shift since right after nursing school.

Didn't get much sleep last night... And I didn't nap long today...

My friend says her doctor gives her Modafinil on the nights she must work the graveyard shift. Not sure I am ready to resort to drugs...

Okay, venti Starbucks. Here we go...

I do love the night shift crew. They are chill compared to us uptight day shift crew - ha!

At eleven, the lights go down in the halls. Nice - ambiance! Just hope it doesn't make me sleepy. Time for more coffee—hospital-grade this time.

Yuck.

Three AM lull—not only is it the time of night when my circadian rhythm slows down, but it is also slow on the unit. Great... Suddenly, my prayer life ramps up.

God, please help me get through the next four hours. Lord, I could use some extra help right now passing 4 am meds.

I need toothpicks for the eyelids. Crunching ice, speed walking the halls, laughing with the CNA, peeking into my patients' rooms more than necessary to see if they need anything, slapping my cheeks - these are what are keeping me awake right now.

Ah, a new admit! Does that make me happy or unhappy? I'm so tired, but it does give me something to do.

Ha! Nailed the IV even though my vision is blurry. Thank goodness for checklists in charting, making sure I don't forget anything.

I don't think I could do ER at night - those guys must be on their toes for 10% of the time and are dealing with ear infections and flu the other 90% of the time.

Day shift - yay! Please hurry in the locker room, please hurry in the locker room, please hurry in the locker room...

Okay, now quick report, quick report, quick report... Yes!

Ah, going home finally!

What a blessing to be reminded to be thankful for one another. Don't we spend enough time complaining about the "other" shift. Aren't we glad they enjoy working those horrendous hours? I think the Lord laughs at us when we complain - "Guess what? Your next call shift is gone be nuts!" (I don't really think He says that, but He should!)

Thank You, God, that I made it through this shift. I did not kill anyone. I did not fall asleep in a corner of the bathroom. God, bless the night shift crew/day shift crew. Help me to be patient and understanding next time I take report from them. Now, can you please help me to wind down and go to sleep? Amen!

Connected with Jesus

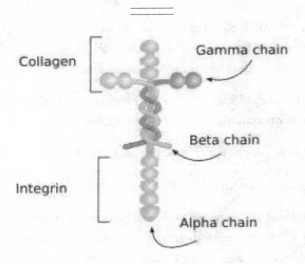

QUICK VERSES FOR THE nurses' lounge: Colossians 1:16-17 – "For in Him all things were created; things in heaven and on earth, visible and invisible, whether thrones or powers or rulers or authorities; all things have been created through Him and for Him. He is before all things, and in Him all things hold together." (New International Version)

For further study later: Psalms 139

The longer I study both human anatomy and God's Word, the more I am astounded by how they complement each other. Just like psychology is proving things God said long ago, the more we know about the human body the more we see that God placed clues to His plan in everyday physiology.

For example, there is a human connective tissue called laminin. It literally holds us together and it is in the shape of a cross!

As is noted in the article <u>Biochemistry of Collagens, Laminins, and Elastins</u>, written by D. Gulager Kring Rasmussen, 2016:

> *Laminins are a major constituent of the basement membrane, which is an intricate meshwork of proteins, separating the epithelium, mesothelium, and endothelium from connective*
>
> *tissue...The essential role of laminins in the basement membrane can be summarized by the following; **Even the most exceptional construction will not last on a poor foundation.*** (Emphasis mine)

When I first saw this fact, I was blown away. Christ is our firm foundation, the cornerstone holding us together. Even down to our very connective tissue!

Another amazing thing noted in the Word is the day that neonatal boys are circumcised – day eight. Leviticus 12:3 states "Then on the eighth day the flesh of his foreskin shall be circumcised."

Why would God make that the day of circumcision? Science tells us why, long after Moses wrote these words in the Torah.

Some amount of decreased platelet count is normal in the newborn after delivering, due to the birth process. However, in the second week of life the platelet count begins to rise again, in a healthy baby. (<u>Neonatal</u>

Thrombocytopenia: Etiology and Diagnosis, Laura Sillers, MD, Charles Van Slambrouck, MD, and Gabrielle Lapping-Carr, MD) Therefore, there will be less chance of hemorrhage on the eighth day of life, when the Jewish *bris* ceremony for circumcision is performed!

As an aside, not necessarily due to anything scientific I have found (yet!), but the Jewish mother is considered ceremonially unclean through day seven.

What does this mean? Well, she can't go to synagogue or anywhere until then. She is just alone with her and her baby – and midwives, who were many times family members – until then. Just peace and quiet, time to feed and bathe and sing and cry and learn to be a new mother. Perhaps this was God's precious provision just for Mom! Isn't He good?

Lord, You are so wise! All of creation tells of You, from the stars to the very cells of our body. As it says in Psalm 139, "I praise You because I am fearfully and wonderfully made... My frame was not hidden from you when I was made in the secret place, when I was woven together in the depths of the earth." Thank You for all the ways You mold me and shape me. Thank You for Your care and precise engineering. May I never stop learning of all Your goodness to me. Amen.

No Luck Involved

QUICK VERSE FOR THE nurses' lounge: "He has saved us and called us to a holy life- not because of anything we have done but because of his own purpose and grace. This grace was given us in Christ Jesus before the beginning of time." (New International Version)

For further study later: Romans 12

What a ride this life as a nurse is! We meet interesting people, and we learn how to deal with difficult people. We save lives and we watch some lives slip into eternity. We develop not only as a health care practitioner, but also our own character – setting priorities, learning time management, learning people management, and understanding our limitations. We fall down and we get back up. We encourage our colleagues, and we sometimes discourage our colleagues.

Nurses are a superstitious lot, amiright? We groan if anyone uses the Q word. We insist that a full moon makes a difference in admissions or acuity or levels of crazy in our patients. We just know that the patients can sense when we sit down to eat and call for us right then. We feel "lucky" if the shift was –quiet. We feel unlucky if we get *that* OR to circulate. Some bad stuff happens in there!

But, deep down, we all know we are blessed. We felt called to this profession.

We sweated and cried through nursing school. We took a deep breath, wiped our sweaty palms on our scrubs, and stepped through the door of our first job. We gritted our teeth when the doctor or manager gave us a good old-fashioned scolding, whether we deserved it or not.

We teared up at our first delivery. We fainted at our first surgery.

Even now, we almost fall asleep driving home and we for sure don't always know how we made it home after a shift! We love some patients and can't stand others. We love some co-workers and can't stand others.

Our experiences and settings as nurses vary. Some of us remain staff nurses for our entire career. Some of us go on to management or CRNA or NP.

Some of us work in a hospital, some in a doctor's office, and some even from our car, driving here and there, caring for homebound patients.

The one constant for all of us is we are proud of our profession. If some bozo says that must be the doctor's stethoscope or says we just sit around and play cards all shift, we come out en masse and prove just how valuable we are. We suck it up in the middle of a worldwide pandemic and dive right in. We volunteer to sub for our kid's school nurse, we run/walk in March of Dimes walks, and we go on medical mission trips on our "vacations."

But we wouldn't change it. Maybe change where we practice, but not our whole profession.

An unfortunate closing of labor and delivery happened at my long-term workplace recently. Although I had already left, I grieved for my former colleagues and friends. It was heart-wrenching.

Yet God was faithful. Most of them love their new places even more! Many went to a hospital system that appreciates their nurses more. Some moved into management, some moved into home health care, and some decided to stay home full-time. Some even retired!

All would tell you that they love nursing. Not everything about it, of course.

But it is a good life. A fulfilling life. A rewarding life. An exhausting life.

Sometimes I feel that we as nurses need to take a step back and remember all the good things about our profession, when we are tempted to complain. We love being nurses.

Lord, you have blessed me with this profession. That is why I tell my kids to marry nurses, even if they decide not to become one! I know you called me to this job. I pray for all the future nurses – for passion for their job, for joy in the journey, and for good shifts. Amen.

Note from the author

THANK YOU TO MY READERS. I hope you have enjoyed spending time in the Word and prayer in these pages as much as I have enjoyed writing them. May your patients be kind, your managers patient, and your shifts – Never mind. I started to say the Q word.

Thank you to two amazing "editor" friends. First, Leslie Caro, the kind of nurse I want to be and the kind of teacher I want my sons to have. She helped me both with editorial and nurse-related issues. Next, Bethany McMillon, my kids' librarian, and an author herself. She ensured that I followed the writing rules and helped make my wording clearer. I love you both!

To my present and former co-workers, except for one scene with a doctor, all the other scenes have been adjusted and/or names changed to protect the innocent.

Of course, a huge debt of gratitude goes to my husband and my boys who took care of themselves on many Tuesday nights when I escaped to the library to write.

And to my friend Jesus – it is all in Your honor. May You be glorified.

Jennifer

Photo credits

Cover image: Vladimir Fedotov

Page 1: Stacey Gabrielle Koenitz Rozells

Page 7: Evan Wise

Page 15: Luis Melendez

Page 18: Jonathan Borba

Page 34: National Cancer

Page 54: Atlantios

Page 57: Beyond My Ken

Page 62: Thomas Perkins

the rest are either my own, or from royalty-free photo pages

Don't miss out!

Visit the website below and you can sign up to receive emails whenever Jennifer Goolsby publishes a new book. There's no charge and no obligation.

https://books2read.com/r/B-A-BMWR-ZLKWB

BOOKS 2 READ

Connecting independent readers to independent writers.

About the Author

Jennifer Goolsby has worked in healthcare as a nurse for over 25 years. She began in pediatrics nursing and has worked since in surgical nursing and labor and delivery. She has been published in numerous ezines and she writes on daytodaygraces.com about being a nurse while raising three grown and almost-grown boys. Her loves of nursing and parenting are only beaten by her love of sharing Jesus through life stories - after all, He taught through stories, too!

Read more at https://daytodaygraces.com/.

9 798201 432140